eco GUIDES

A Teen Guide to

Being Eco in Your Community

Cath Senker

Raintree

Raintree is an imprint of Capstone Global Library Limited, a company incorporated in England and Wales having its registered office at 7 Pilgrim Street, London, EC4V 6LB – Registered company number: 6695582

www.raintreepublishers.co.uk
myorders@raintreepublishers.co.uk

Text © Capstone Global Library Limited 2013
First published in hardback in 2013
Paperback edition first published in 2014
The moral rights of the proprietor have been asserted.

Edited by Andrew Farrow, Adam Miller, and
  Vaarunika Dharmapala
Designed by Richard Parker
Original illustrations © Capstone Global Library
  Ltd 2013
Illustrated by HL Studios
Picture research by Tracy Cummins
Originated by Capstone Global Library Ltd
Printed and bound in China by CTPS

ISBN 978 1 406 24983 5 (hardback)
16 15 14 13 12
10 9 8 7 6 5 4 3 2 1

ISBN 978 1 406 24988 0 (paperback)
17 16 15 14 13
10 9 8 7 6 5 4 3 2 1

British Library Cataloguing in Publication Data
Senker, Cath.
A teen guide to being eco in your community. -- (Eco guides)
363.7'0525-dc23
A full catalogue record for this book is available from the British Library.

Acknowledgements
We would like to thank the following for permission to reproduce photographs: Alamy pp. 9 (© David J. Green – electrical), 11 top (© Construction Photography), 20 (© Anthony Pleva), 22, 23 (© Jeff Greenberg), 25 (© Peter Titmuss); Capstone Library pp. 43, 45, 47 (Karon Dubke); Corbis pp. 21 (© Reuters), 34 (© Tim Pannell); Getty Images pp. 5 (Echo), 6 (Mark D Callanan), 10 (Photo Researchers), 13 (AARON MAASHO/AFP), 15 (KidStock), 31 (Andrew Holt), 41 (Jupiterimages); LA Photo Party p. 33 (Brian Miller); Lothrop Science, Spanish, Technology Magnet Omaha Public Schools p. 36 (Pamela Galus); Shutterstock pp.4 (Dmitriy Shironosov), 8 (Kuramyndra), 11 (bottom) (manfredxy), 14 (Nikola Spasenoski), 29 (left) (Zoran Vukmanov Simokov), 29 (right) (gillmar), 30 (rangizzz), 32 (AVAVA), 35 (Andre Blais), 38 (jabiru), 39 (Leftleg), 40 (monticello), 48 (Claus Mikosch), 49 (Inc); Superstock pp. 7 (© imagebroker.net), 12 (© Belinda Images), 26, 37 (© Ambient Images Inc.).

Cover photograph of a couple working in a garden reproduced with permission of Corbis (© Mika). Cover logo of eco sticker reproduced with permission of Shutterstock (Olivier Le Moal).

Every effort has been made to contact copyright holders of material reproduced in this book. Any omissions will be rectified in subsequent printings if notice is given to the publisher.

Contents

Some words are shown in bold, **like this**. You can find out what they mean by looking in the glossary.

Important!

Please check with an adult before doing the projects in this book.

How can I be eco?

We all know that human activities have a huge impact on our environment, from using up the world's resources to affecting **climate change**. We realize it makes sense to reduce that impact as much as we can. Although the problems may seem vast, every one of us can make a difference. It's easy to get started – there are many quick, simple, and cheap things we can all do.

This book considers how you can be eco in your community. So, who *are* your community? They are the people around you – your neighbours and people in local shops, places of worship, and schools. Sports and outdoor activity clubs, Scouts, and music or dance organizations are also communities.

We benefit from being part of one or many communities just as we thrive from having friends and family around us. If any of the communities you belong to are not already involved in eco actions, they might be interested in adopting some eco ideas. As well as helping the environment, it may save them money!

The girls at this dance club could consider making the lighting more eco friendly.

Meeting neighbours

Zocalo is a small community scheme in Brighton. Once a year, people are encouraged to get to know their neighbours by putting a couple of chairs on the pavement outside their house. People wander up and down the street, sharing food and drink. At simple events like these, the seeds of community projects can be planted. At one Zocalo event, a group of neighbours decided to set up a communal compost heap.

The range of issues to tackle may seem bewildering – from saving energy and water, reducing waste, and environmentally friendly food, to encouraging nature and **biodiversity**. So, why not consider where you could most easily make changes, and start from there? This book has realistic projects you can do right now, with a little help from others in your community. Millions of people all over the world are doing these things. So, what are you waiting for?

The sky's the limit: wind turbines

Local eco groups may be able to build up to ambitious projects. Wausau East High School in Wisconsin, USA, has installed its own **wind turbine** to produce energy. The wind turbine provides about 5 per cent of the school's power needs, saving about £9,100 a year on electricity bills.

This teacher and pupils are discussing how wind power works.

What's in it for me?

By promoting and protecting nature, you can make the places where you live, study, and socialize more pleasant. You could help your family save money by reducing energy bills. If you can help reduce costs significantly, your parent or carer might reward you!

Why be eco at school?

Your school is a ready-made community so it's an easy place to start being eco. It can be good for your education, too. Working in the fresh air on outdoor gardening and nature projects makes a welcome change from sitting in a classroom. Seeing the results of your work provides great motivation to continue. Imagine spotting the first winged visitors to your nature area or harvesting your home-grown vegetables!

People all around the world enjoy nature. Here, residents of Jalisco, Mexico are celebrating the arrival of spring.

New friends, new skills

If you become more involved in your school and local community, you'll make friends with people of different ages and backgrounds as well as gain useful skills. The ability to co-operate with a variety of people and to organize activities will look good on your CV when you apply for college, university, or jobs.

This vegetable patch grows in an urban garden in Detroit, Michigan, USA. You don't have to live in the country to go green!

"By taking the concept of **sustainable** living beyond the narrow, individualistic [focused on individuals] approach, we can learn to see our interconnectedness to our environment and its inhabitants. By getting involved in our communities, by talking to our neighbors, by supporting local groups, and by re-imagining where we live, we can green not only our own lifestyles, but our streets, neighborhoods, towns, cities and, ultimately, our societies. Who knows, we may even make friends doing it."

Sami Grover, writer and environmental activist, North Carolina, USA

Eco jobs

If you enjoy being eco in your community, you may decide to pursue a career in environmental work. Here are a few possible occupations:

- Environmental **conservation** involves managing parks and countryside recreation areas, waste management, and the protection of wild birds.
- Forestry includes the management of trees, forests, and woodlands.
- Within businesses, environmental officers are responsible for improving **energy efficiency** and waste management.
- **Non-governmental organizations** need people to undertake practical conservation, educate the public, and campaign on specific issues.
- Newspapers and television programmes need writers and researchers who are knowledgable about the environment.

YOUR COMMUNITY: Energy, water, and waste

Reducing energy and water use and reducing the waste we produce may sound like huge tasks, but there are several simple eco actions you can easily adopt at home or your sports clubhouse, school, community centre, or place of worship. They will soon become habits. When many individuals work together, you can make a real difference.

Save energy, save money

Take the challenge and adopt these simple ideas for saving energy:

- Accept that it's cold in winter! Do you really need to keep your home as hot as a sauna so you can go round in a T-shirt? Embrace winter by wearing a warm, cosy jumper.
- You tend to feel cold when you are sitting still. Instead of turning up the heating when you're watching TV or using the computer, consider snuggling up with a soft blanket around you.
- Don't stand by! It's effortless to switch off appliances when you stop using them so you don't leave them guzzling energy on standby. See if you can borrow an energy monitor (see panel on page 9) to check how much energy your household is using. Then see if you could reduce it.

Snuggling up in a blanket to read can be a real pleasure.

Energy monitors

Energy monitors allow you to check how much electricity your appliances are using. The simplest ones can be connected to an appliance. There are also small wireless monitors with a transmitter (device that sends electronic signals) to connect around the cable of your electricity meter. Some energy monitors can store data, which you upload to a computer. All provide useful information about the running costs of your appliances. Try checking how much energy you are currently using at bedtime. In fact, almost every appliance except the fridge can be turned off!

Keep cool, avoid waste

When it's hot in summer, it's tempting to crank up the air conditioning or switch on fans to keep cool. But there are ways to reduce the heat without using up large amounts of energy. For example, did you know that direct sunlight on a window can produce as much heat as a radiator? To cut out heat, close blinds and curtains during the hottest part of the day. Open the windows in the cool of the morning and the evening to lower the temperature. Electrical appliances and lights produce heat as well as light, so it's sensible to turn them off when not in use.

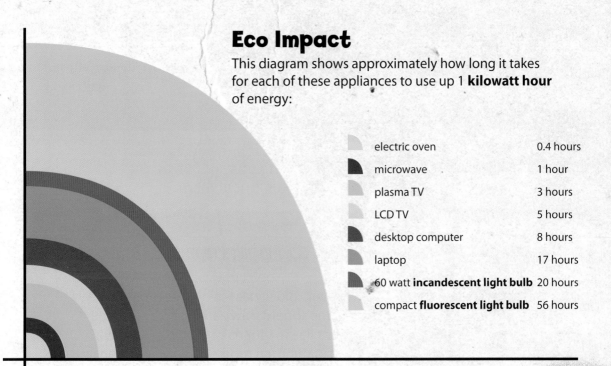

Eco Impact

This diagram shows approximately how long it takes for each of these appliances to use up 1 **kilowatt hour** of energy:

electric oven	0.4 hours
microwave	1 hour
plasma TV	3 hours
LCD TV	5 hours
desktop computer	8 hours
laptop	17 hours
60 watt **incandescent light bulb**	20 hours
compact **fluorescent light bulb**	56 hours

Eco groups can help!

If you're part of a group of like-minded people, they'll support you to change your habits and stick to greener ways. For help finding a group, try www.ecoteams.org.uk.

Eco scouts

In the United States, the Scouting Movement is going eco. In 2011, they introduced eco-friendly Scout jerseys. The jerseys are made from Repreve, a recyclable wool produced using water bottles made of PET (a type of plastic). Normal sportswear is made from synthetic fabrics which use crude oil. Every 450 grams (1 pound) of Repreve used saves 1.9 litres (0.5 gallons) of oil.

Some eco groups use technology to help people work out how to save energy. In the United Kingdom, the Three Villages Eco Group carries out **thermal imaging** to show people where heat is escaping from their homes. To minimize heat loss from the doors and windows, the residents can put in **draught proofing** and line their curtains.

In this thermogram of a home in winter, the red areas show where heat is escaping.

Be clean and green

The way we wash has a major impact on our water usage. Don't worry – you can be squeaky clean and eco friendly, too! If you usually have a bath, how about having a refreshing five-minute shower instead?

Bear in mind that some power showers use even more water than the average bath, and that having a long shower may have the same effect as having a bath!

To ensure you can have a great shower while still using water responsibly, why not talk to your family about buying a water-saving shower head? This small device reduces the flow of water but you can still enjoy a powerful shower. It's quite cheap to buy and soon saves money on your hot water bill. It will also reduce the amount of water that has to be extracted from rivers and the ground.

You can fit a water **flow restrictor** (shown left) to every tap in your house to reduce the amount of water you use.

Save water

- Check the dishwasher or washing machine is full before you run it. Are you using the most efficient energy and water settings?
- Try using a sinkful of water to wash up a large pile of dishes twice a day rather than washing up every time you have a snack or drink.
- While you're waiting for the water to run hot when you're doing the washing up, you could fill up a bowl with cooler water for rinsing.
- If you boil just the water you need in the kettle, you'll save energy and your drink will be ready quickly.
- When you're washing your hands or face, pop in the plug and run just the water you need.
- You could pour left-over glasses of water on your plants.

How to tackle waste

It's not hard to reduce, reuse, and recycle and still have everything you need! Some people like to add a fourth "R" – refuse to purchase. Before you buy something, think carefully about whether you really need it. For example, you might want access to a product but you don't really need to own it. You can read the latest magazines and newspapers in a library for free. It's also free to borrow library books, and cheap to hire CDs and DVDs. For the purchases you do need, invest in a durable shopping bag so you can avoid coming home clutching plastic bags.

When you shop, try to find items made from recycled material.

Swap or sell

Reusing goods is simple, too. See if you can join a Freecycle group in your area. People give away goods they no longer need rather than throwing them in the bin. (Check with a parent before you join and always go with a trusted adult to collect items.) Or why not hold a car boot sale and sell those old toys, games, and clothes? You will learn some bargaining skills and hopefully make some money.

Buying second-hand products is another great idea. How about investing in some retro clothing? An interesting, original item from a charity shop will help you stand out from the crowd.

Recycling

You probably already recycle paper, card, and plastic. Did you know that you can also recycle household items such as batteries, CDs, DVDs, and light bulbs? Check your local council website to find out where to take them. Of course, it's no use recycling unless people buy the new goods produced, so look out for interesting products made from recycled materials.

Eco Impact

Tyres are tough, resistant to chemicals, and do not melt. They are made from nylon fabrics and metal, covered with hard rubber. Once they have worn down, car users have to replace them. In the United Kingdom, about 25 million tyres are thrown away each year. One company, Remarkable, shreds used tyres into tiny pieces and turns them into a smooth, flexible sheet. This sheet is made into pencil cases, mouse mats, and notepads.

This woman runs a successful business in Ethiopia, making shoes from recycled tyres and fabrics.

Being green - summing up

- Save energy by wearing cosy clothing at home.
- Turn off appliances when not in use.
- Have quick showers to stay clean and fresh.
- Use just the water you need.
- Keep reducing, reusing, and recycling.

Nature and biodiversity

How can you make your neighbourhood nature-friendly? Perhaps there's a nature club in your area that you could join. Otherwise, why not gather some friends and neighbours together to encourage wildlife to your local area?

You can plant herbs and wild flowers to attract beneficial (helpful) insects such as butterflies, bees, and ladybirds. Bees and butterflies **pollinate** plants, while ladybirds feed on aphids (small insects that damage plants). Make sure the varieties you choose are suitable for your local climate. These are all quite easy to grow:

Herbs: Basil, Borage, Dill, Fennel, Lavender, Parsley, Thyme, Sage

Flowers: Cornflower, Clematis, Hydrangea, Mexican Hat, Zinnia

Eco Impact

One-third of the human diet can be traced to bee pollination. Bees pollinate crops, so they can be fertilized and reproduce. Bee populations have dwindled, but it's easy to create a bee-friendly environment. In Stirling, Scotland, the On the Verge project asks schools and community groups to plant wild flowers and **nectar-rich** plants in the spring to help the bee population recover.

As these bees fly among the buttercups and daisies, they will pollinate both types of flower. Encouraging bees does not mean you will get stung, as long as you are careful.

These volunteers are planting a tree. Once it's in the soil, they will add **mulch** and water it.

Attracting the right visitors

There's nothing worse than planting herbs and flowers only to find they have been munched by insects. Luckily, there are several ways to encourage beneficial insects and deter harmful ones naturally, without harming wildlife or the environment. A popular method is companion planting – combining plants that help each other by deterring pests. For example, plant chives, garlic, or coriander to repel aphids. Dill attracts beneficial insects such as hoverflies and wasps that eat aphids. Find out more at www.bbc.co.uk/gardening/basics/techniques/organic_companionplanting1.shtml.

The benefits of trees

Trees play an important role in our environment. In urban areas, they attract wildlife, and provide greenery and shade in summer. In places that are prone to flooding, they retain water and reduce the run-off of water. The School Tree Nursery Programme helps school children to plant trees to improve their local habitat. The children help to raise the saplings within the school grounds, and once they are big enough, they plant them out in the community. In Lewes, East Sussex, for instance, trees have been planted on the **floodplain** to try to reduce the harmful effects of future flooding by local rivers.

Attracting birds

You could make a small nest box with a hole to attract tit species and sparrows. It's wise to find out the kinds of birds that nest locally so you make the right kind of home for them. For information, try www.bto.org/nnbw/which.htm.

Why make a nest box?

Many bird species depend on holes in trees and buildings to make their nest. These sites disappear when woods and gardens are tidied, and people repair old houses. Nest boxes can help make up for the loss.

Putting up your nest box

Attach your box at the end of winter, using galvanized (rust-proof) or stainless-steel nails. Check that it will be sheltered from the **prevailing wind**, rain, and strong sunlight. The front of the nest should be angled slightly downwards to prevent rain from dripping into it. Either put the box 1–3 metres (3–10 feet) above the ground on a tree, on a wall, or on the side of a shed. Check that predators such as cats or squirrels cannot easily reach the nest. Also check that it is not near bird feeders so visiting birds won't disturb the nesting birds. For more information, go to www.bto.org/nnbw/essentials.htm.

Make a nest box for birds

You will need:

Plank of wood 15 cm x 117 cm (6 x 46 in) and at least 1.5 cm (0.6 in) thick. (It's sensible to allow a little extra in case something goes wrong.)
Saw
Drill
Pencil
Galvanized or stainless-steel nails
Waterproof material such as car tyre inner tube or Butyl rubber to make the hinge

Please ask an adult to supervise this project.

Method:

1. Saw the parts to the sizes shown in the diagram.

2. Drill small holes in the base piece to drain out rainwater.

3. Drill a hole in the front piece. It should be:

   2.5 cm (1 in) or larger for a Blue, Coal, or Marsh tit

   2.8 cm (1.1 in) or larger for a Great tit or Tree sparrow

   3.2 mm (1.3 in) for a House sparrow

4. Drill a hole in the back piece to attach the nest box.

5. Mark in pencil where the sides, roof, and base will fit on to the back piece.

6. Cut a groove in the back piece where the roof will slot in. Make sure the roof fits snugly.

7. Nail the sides to the back piece, then nail on the base.

8. Nail the front to the sides and base.

9. Make a hinge to attach the roof. First, cut the rubber to the width of the box. Then nail the rubber along the back of the box and to the roof. Finally, attach the box to a tree.

Source: National Nest Box Week, www.bto.org/nnbw/index.htm

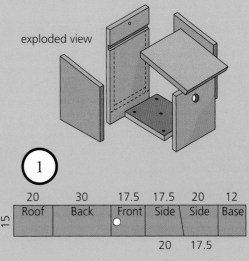

exploded view

①

	20	30	17.5	17.5	20	12
15	Roof	Back	Front	Side	Side	Base
					20	17.5

plank size 15cm x 117cm

③ ⑥

groove

⑦

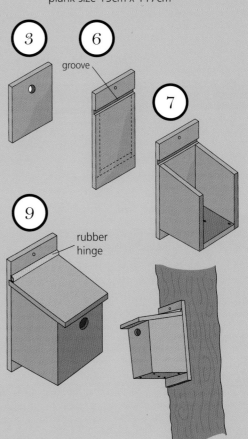

⑨

rubber hinge

Attracting wildlife

A small pond is a wonderful way to attract wildlife. Before you start, there are some points to consider. Can you position your pond away from overhanging trees and in partial shade? You'll need to think about the shape of your pond. It should have shallow areas to allow creatures to get in and out easily, and birds to bathe. It's important to get the right balance of plants, too.

Build a small pond

You will need:

Spade
Pond liner, bought from a garden centre or online (try to buy one that is
   recycled or made from rubber). Use this formula to work out how much you
   need: (length + [depth x 2]) + (width + [depth x 2]). For example, if your
   pond is 2.5 m (8 ft) long by 1.5 m (5 ft) wide, and 1 m (3 ft) deep, you'll need:
   2.5 + 2 + 1.5 + 2 m = 8 m (8 + 6 + 5 + 6 ft = 25 ft) of pond liner.
Soft sand
A few rocks
Long grass seed (optional)
Plants

Please ask an adult to supervise this project.

Method:

1. Measure out the area of the pond.

2. Dig the hole. Start with a hole at least 80 cm deep (2 ft 7 in) at one end. The other end should come up at a slope of 20°.

3. Remove sharp stones or roots. Leave a step on which to later place shallow water plants.

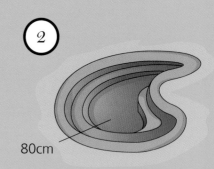

2

80cm

Aquatic plants

Use four types of plants to keep your pond healthy:

- *Oxygenators* keep the water clear. Try water milfoil or willow moss.
- *Floating plants* provide shelter. Try water hyacinth or water lettuce.
- *Marginal plants* provide protection from predators. Try marsh marigolds or water forget-me-nots.
- *Deep-water aquatics* should be planted 30 cm (1 ft) deep or more. Their leaves provide shade and shelter. Try water hawthorn.

Being green - summing up

- Plant herbs and wild flowers to encourage beneficial insects.
- Plant trees to help improve the environment.
- Make a nest box to shelter birds.
- Build a pond to attract wildlife.

4. Add a layer of sand to the pond.

5. Place the pond liner in the hole, allowing for an overlap of 30–50 cm (12–20 in).

6. Place a few rocks around the shallow end. Mammals will be able to lean off them to drink the water.

7. If you'd like to attract frogs, plant some long grass seed around the deep end to provide shelter from predators and shade from the Sun.

8. If possible, fill the pond with rainwater. Otherwise, use tap water, but leave it for two weeks before adding plants to allow any chemicals to evaporate.

9. Add some aquatic (water-living) plants.

10. Cover the edge of the liner, to protect it, for example with turf or slate.

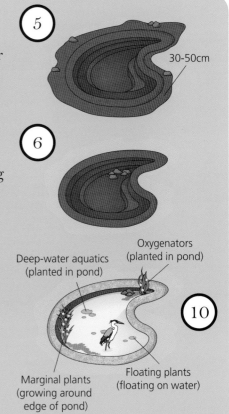

5 — 30-50cm

6

Deep-water aquatics (planted in pond)

Oxygenators (planted in pond)

10

Marginal plants (growing around edge of pond)

Floating plants (floating on water)

A healthy neighbourhood

Is your local area a mess? It's not hard to improve it a little. Simple tasks such as making posters to persuade people to use rubbish bins or to clean up dog mess can help your neighbours to clean up their act. It's also worth reminding people that it's illegal to drop litter and that they can be fined for doing so. You could even get together with friends to organize a litter pick (see page 23), plant some herbs, or encourage more walking and cycling.

Does this sound unrealistic? Well, it has been shown that people make the choice whether to litter, so putting up notices to focus attention on the issue can make a real difference. Keep Australia Beautiful ran a competition to create a 30-second advert with an anti-littering message aimed at under-25s. Robbie Reid was one of the young people who took up the challenge. He produced an anti-litter advert with a cute animated crab called Kevin, who advised viewers to "stash trash" in the bin. Robbie won an award of AUD$1,000 (£650)!

Much of this rubbish could have been recycled. You can see paper, card, a can, and plastic bottles. The plastic bags could have been reused.

Littering: the facts

Keep America Beautiful carried out a survey of littering and discovered that:

- Nearly one in five people (17 per cent) dropped litter in a public place, while most (83 per cent) disposed of it properly.
- People are more likely to litter if the area is already littered. In contrast, if there are recycling and rubbish bins handy, people tend to use them.
- Littering is an individual choice. People who believe littering is wrong use the bins. Individuals can encourage others not to litter and help to change habits.

A herb patch

Once you've tackled the rubbish … how about community food growing? Is there a patch of unused ground in your area? If you are part of a community eco group, you could seek permission from your local council to plant some herbs for everyone to use. Or perhaps a local place of worship has a space where you could grow plants in pots. It is easy to do, and your cooking will be tastier with fresh herbs.

Rooftop gardens

Tokyo, Japan, is a densely populated city. Few people have gardens. In recent years, however, people have developed an interest in growing their own food. As space is an issue, these gardeners are ingenious, creating vegetable plots in front of railway stations and making rooftop gardens. Businesses have become involved, too. For example, in 2011 East Japan Railway opened a rental garden on the rooftop of the Lumine Ogikubo Building. People can rent plots to grow fruit and vegetables, as well as use the garden to relax and socialize.

Litter

Is there an area near you that is ruined by litter? Why not organize a litter pick? You could start with a small clean-up, for example, on your school fields. Perhaps you could ask pupils, parents, and teachers to sponsor you to raise the money you'll need for equipment.

These volunteers in Little Haiti (above) and Baynanza Biscayne Bay (page 23), both in Miami, Florida, USA, are taking part in a community day to clean up their neighbourhoods.

Stay safe!

It's important to find an adult to supervise your event in case you find dangerous materials. Make sure everyone in your group knows that if they spot syringes, they should not touch them. Syringes can cause injury or infection. After the litter pick, contact your local council and tell them where you found the materials.

Organize a community litter pick

Here's how to plan your litter pick:

1. Find some friends to form an organizing group, and an adult to support you.

2. You may need to get permission to work in your chosen area. Ask an adult to help you to check about **public liability insurance**.

3. Pick a day and time for the event. Two hours should be enough.

4. Publicize the event. You could tell the local media.

5. With an adult, carry out a **risk assessment** of the area. There may be hazards, such as broken glass, or syringes.

6. Find equipment. You can ask everyone to bring strong gloves and bin bags. You'll also need litter grabbers, and luminous jackets if possible. It's helpful to have some bags and containers to store sharp objects, and tape to seal them. Make sure you have a first aid kit. You may be able to get some equipment for free from Keep Britain Tidy (www. keepbritaintidy.org).

7. Work out how to dispose of the litter afterwards. For example, you could separate recyclable and non-recyclable materials into different-coloured bin bags. If there's not too much, you can put out the rubbish and recycling with your household bin. If there's a lot, you may need to arrange for your local council to pick it up or take it to your local waste and recycling centre.

8. Celebrate your work! It's worth taking "before" and "after" photos and sending them to the media. If you've done well, you're bound to get plenty of support for your next litter pick.

Source: LitterAction, www.litteraction.org.uk

Get on your bike!

We all know that vehicles use up precious **fossil fuels** and create air pollution. But how easy is it to change how you travel? Maybe you could start with a small change in your habits, such as replacing one journey a week in a vehicle by cycling or walking.

Cycling and walking

Pros
- Cycling and walking are good for your health.
- Cycling is cheap and walking costs nothing.
- The more people walk or cycle, the less traffic there is on the roads.
- Many towns and cities have bike lanes, often making it faster to use a bike than a car.
- On a bike, you can zip through traffic and park in many places.
- If you enjoy nature, you are more likely to spot interesting plants and animals than you would in a car.
- Cycling is a popular and sociable sport.
- Your bike needs regular maintenance to keep it in good working order but it is quite simple once you know how.

Cons
- Cycling or walking may not be practical for long distances.
- Road traffic can make it dangerous to cycle.
- Traffic fumes can make it unpleasant to walk or cycle.
- Many people feel unsafe walking or cycling in the dark.
- Not every climate is suitable for year-round cycling or walking. For safety, cyclists need to invest in good wet-weather gear and high-visibility clothing such as a bib or vest with reflective strips.

Eco Impact

In the United States in 2008, just 0.5 per cent of journeys to work were made by bike, while under 3 per cent were made on foot. However, there was an increase in cycling to work of 43 per cent between 2000 and 2008. This shows that habits can change over time.

Cycle safety

So, how can cycling be encouraged? Some simple changes can make a difference. It's helpful to have bike racks or other safe storage areas for bicycles at school, sports clubs, and other places in the community. Spreading knowledge about bike maintenance and safety is useful, too.

If you get involved in promoting cycling or any other eco project in your community, see if you can hold an event to promote your work, and get more people involved.

Transport survey

Ask your friends about the transport they use, how often they use it, and the distances they travel. Work out the average distance people walk or cycle, and how often. Ask what it would take to persuade them to walk or cycle more and further. Which key factors would help? Repeat the survey to see if you are having an impact on the behaviour of your friends.

Being green - summing up

- Organize a litter pick to tidy up your local area.
- Put up posters to deter littering.
- Create a community garden.
- Replace some journeys with cycling or walking.

Cycling is an easy, gentle exercise. It helps to improve your fitness which can reduce your risk of health problems in later life.

YOUR SCHOOL: Saving energy and water

Why would you want to be eco-friendly at school? Firstly, you spend a lot of time there, so you'll benefit if the school environment improves. Secondly, a school is a large community, so eco-friendly measures can make a real difference. Thirdly, eco projects allow you to become more involved in the running of your school.

Eco-Schools

Has your school joined the worldwide Eco-Schools Network? It enables you to share ideas and ask for advice. For example, Slovakian schoolchildren visited Berlin and Hamburg schools in 2009 and learnt methods for taking responsibility for eco projects.

Eco-Schools Scotland has a forum on its website. One pupil posted a question about how to get others involved in their eco committee. Other pupils suggested handing out fliers, putting up posters, and promoting projects in assembly at the start of term – when people are fresh from their holidays.

This community group are being given a demonstration on how to properly plant a tree.

Start small

Don't worry if your school isn't in the Eco-Schools Network. To kick off some activity, how about finding out if your friends might like to become involved? Then, see if you can find at least one teacher to support your environmental projects. You could set up an eco club or become an eco class. Maybe you can get your school caretaker on board, or the parents through the Parent Teacher Association.

It might be easiest to start by focusing on one theme. For example, at Eco-School Elie Faure de Lormont, France, the pupils focused on waste in the first year, food in the second year, and then biodiversity in the third year.

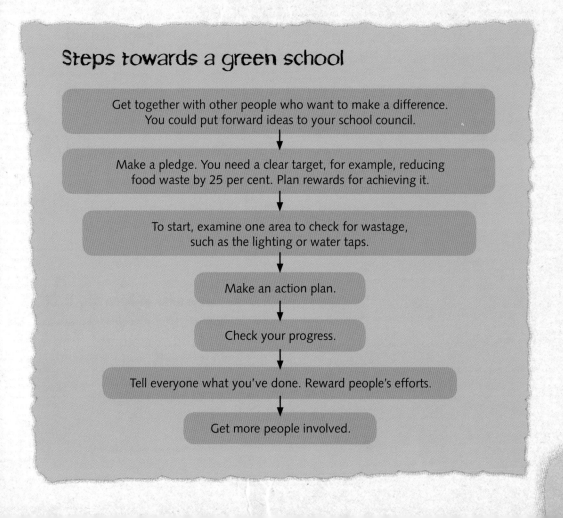

Steps towards a green school

Get together with other people who want to make a difference. You could put forward ideas to your school council.

↓

Make a pledge. You need a clear target, for example, reducing food waste by 25 per cent. Plan rewards for achieving it.

↓

To start, examine one area to check for wastage, such as the lighting or water taps.

↓

Make an action plan.

↓

Check your progress.

↓

Tell everyone what you've done. Reward people's efforts.

↓

Get more people involved.

Easy energy saving

Saving energy is a great idea – but how do you know where you need to cut back? It's worth carrying out an energy review to see how much energy you are using at the moment. This document includes a model you can use: www.ecoschoolsscotland.org/documents/PrimarySecondaryEnvironmentalReview2011.pdf.

The simplest way to cut energy use in schools is to look at lighting. Firstly, you could do a survey of lights left on in empty rooms. Also look at lighting levels. You need different levels of lighting for different tasks, for example, corridors require far less than classrooms or science labs. Some areas may have too much or too little light. You could carry out a similar survey for radiators. Are they being left on in unused rooms? Are some areas too hot or too cold?

Energy action plan

Next, work on your action plan. Start with easy actions, such as putting up notices reminding people to turn off lights when they are not needed. Studies have shown that natural light in classrooms is good for your health and helps you to learn better. So, if it's a bright day, you can switch off the lights. Another simple step is to change the light bulbs for energy-efficient ones. Have a chat with the school caretaker about this. You could also check whether the lights and heating are turned off during weekends and school holidays.

Energy-efficient light bulbs

Cheap energy-efficient light bulbs may seem like a bargain. However, they may not be as efficient as the top brands and won't save you money in the long run. Here's where a bit of maths comes in handy. You can buy a light bulb for £3.60 that has a rated life of 850 hours. The alternative is a bulb that produces the same light for 18,000 hours but costs £40. Energy use is the same for each bulb. Which bulb is a better buy? Check your answer on page 55.

Remember to be patient with the people you are trying to persuade. Explain the benefits of your proposals clearly and allow them time to make a decision. Here's an example you could mention: Sleepy Hollow Middle School in Sleepy Hollow, New York, USA, came up with a cheap, simple way to cut energy. They connected all their computers to a power strip. This made it effortless to switch them all off at the mains at the end of the day.

How long do different light sources last?

light source	efficiency (lumens/watt)	average life (hours)
standard incandescent	5–20	750–1,000
tungsten-halogen	15–25	2,000–4,000
compact fluorescent (5–26 watts)	20–55	10,000
compact fluorescent (27–40 watts)	50–80	15,000–20,000

Compact fluorescent bulbs can replace traditional incandescent bulbs in many light fixtures. Halogen lamps are a type of incandescent lighting but they are more efficient. They are commonly used in floor and desk lamps and for flood lighting.

compact fluorescent

standard incandescent

Progress check

Once you have some energy-saving measures in place, it's sensible to carry out regular reviews to check if usage is being reduced. This involves doing the surveys again. Hopefully, energy use will have decreased. If not, don't despair! Perhaps the message isn't getting across – why not do more publicity for your campaign? If you have managed to reduce usage, celebrate your achievements – then move on to your next campaign!

Ways to cut water waste

Another important area to tackle is water waste. You can adopt the same approach as for energy usage: carry out a review, develop an action plan, do a follow-up review to check progress, and assess if further action is required. Here's a sample water review that you can use: www.ecoschoolsscotland.org/documents/PrimarySecondaryEnvironmentalReview2011.pdf.

Water review

Areas to cover:
- School buildings: find out about water use in all the buildings and calculate the amount of water used per person per day.
- Water-using devices: discover how much water is used, for example, in the toilets, sinks, water fountains, showers, and science labs.
- School grounds: water used for watering the fields or gardens.

Materials you'll need:
- Figures for how much water the school used over the past 12 months or, if possible, the school's water bill
- Stopwatch for calculating the **flow rate** of taps, showers, and water fountains
- **Flow meter bags** or bucket
- Camera for recording observations and presenting results

Checking water flow

Reducing water flow from taps can save water and cut the cost of heating water. The flow rate need not be more than 9 litres (16 pints) per minute. If it's more, you can fix flow restrictors (see page 11) to the taps so the water doesn't come out so fast. To check flow rate:

1. Run water into a flow meter bag or bucket for 15 seconds.
2. Measure the water. Multiply by four to get the flow rate per minute.
3. If it's more than 9 litres per minute, recommend that your school buys flow restrictors.

This Ethiopian girl is transporting water in a heavy container. Many people around the world do not have the luxury of just turning on a tap in their home or school.

Water action!

Once you have carried out a review, brainstorm ideas for an action plan. Many actions cost nothing, or very little. You could make posters to encourage people not to waste water while washing their hands. At SOS Children's Village in Imzouren, Morocco, the children performed a play to inform others about the importance of saving water. You could ask the canteen staff to avoid using trays when possible, to reduce washing up. You'll probably need to talk to the maintenance staff, too. Perhaps there are leaking taps to mend, or they could cut down on using pressure washers to clean public areas.

Being green - summing up

- Become an Eco-School or start an eco club.
- Review water and energy use.
- Develop an action plan to cut usage.
- Check progress and carry out follow-up actions as needed.
- Celebrate what you've achieved!

Cutting waste: simple tips

What are the three Rs at school? Reduce, reuse, recycle! Most school waste is paper, packaging, and food waste. There are simple ways to reduce these kinds of waste and lighten the rubbish bags.

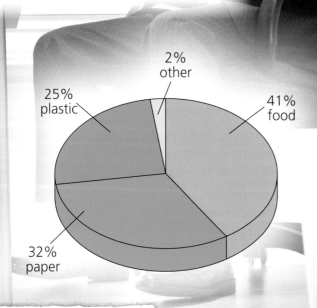

2% other

25% plastic

41% food

32% paper

At Black Mountain School in Scottsdale, Arizona, USA, pupils checked the principal's waste on one day (see pie chart). They then produced a plan to help her recycle more paper and plastic.

Reduce waste

If you have to print out work at school, print double-sided so you use half as much paper. What about litter? One Scottish pupil from an eco group was finding it hard to persuade others to reduce, reuse, and recycle litter. She asked for advice on the Eco-Schools forum. Another pupil replied that at his school pupils receive praise and rewards, such as a special postcard, if they follow the litter policy.

Another worthwhile project is to reduce the use of materials you don't need at all. At Nichols School, New York, USA, the pupils began a movement called Plasti-gone. They aim to persuade schools and businesses not to use single-use plastic products. For example, their "stop sucking" campaign encourages people to stop using drinking straws, which are a waste of resources.

From left to right: Paige Dedrick, Donata Lorenzo, and Caroline Fenn, the girls who started the Plasti-gone movement.

Wipe Out Waste

Around Australia, schools are taking part in the Wipe Out Waste programme. At Unley School, South Australia, pupil Emma Porter started the Environment Group, which set up a card and paper recycling scheme. To help the canteen staff to recycle cardboard, the group bought a trolley so they could transport the cardboard to the collection point. Paper that has been used on only one side is used to make notepads. Unley School also recycles as much plastic as possible.

Reuse

Now you might like to think creatively about how to reuse materials. As always, it's good to start with a survey. Find out how paper is reused. Many goods come in plastic pots – what happens to them once they are empty?

Your eco group could suggest some simple ideas for reusing items. Teachers and pupils can keep paper that has been used on one side for rough work. Plastic pots can serve as containers for pens and pencils. Seedlings can be planted in old drinks cans. When paper cannot be written on any more, try using it for art projects, from papier mâché models to masks. The students at Lyrup Primary School, South Australia, make their waste paper into bricks and sell them to local people for fuel! Here's how they do it: www.wow.sa.gov. au/uploads/pdfdocs/ lyrupfinal.pdf.

Your art department should be able to reuse all kinds of material. Here, papier mâché has been used to make a giant model of the planet Saturn.

Not every school can start a major project such as paper-brick making. So, how can individual pupils reuse materials? A good way is to use lunch boxes and refill water bottles instead of using plastic bags and bottles (see pages 38–39 for ideas).

- In 2008–2009, 12 tonnes (13.2 tons) of waste was diverted from **landfill** every school day by 3,200 Irish schools involved in the Eco-Schools programme.
- 3.7 million units of electricity, 200 million litres (44 million gallons) of drinking water, and around 500,000 litres (109,985 gallons) of fuel were saved in just one year.

Recycle

At the International School of Paris, France, they switched from using bleached white paper to using recycled paper throughout the school. They could recycle the paper again afterwards. This kind of recycling is better for the environment than using a single-use product and chucking it straight in the recycling bin.

Buy a recycled product, such as paper.

Use it fully.

Once you can get no more use out of a product, then it's time to recycle it.

Recycle it.

Reuse the paper wisely.

Drinks in plastic bottles are refrigerated in shops, which uses a large amount of energy. Then resources are used for recycling the bottle – if the user remembers to recycle it! See pages 40–41 for greener alternatives.

Successful school recycling

At Lothrop Science and Technology Magnet School, North Omaha, Nebraska, USA, the pupils take the lead. Older pupils run the recycling programme, passing on their knowledge to younger children.

The project began during a science lesson. The pupils put on masks and thick gloves and emptied the rubbish bins – a disgusting but instructive task! They separated the recyclable materials, and realized many of the materials did not need to go in the bin.

The pupils devised a survey to see how the distance between recycling and rubbish bins affects recycling rates. (People are more likely to recycle if there's a recycling bin to hand.) They discovered that if a recycling monitor stands by the recycling bins at lunchtime, this encourages others to use them.

Now, three pupils each week are on paper patrol. They have 15 minutes to collect recycling from classrooms around the school. In the canteen, pupils sort out the recyclable plastic and collect food waste for composting. They have succeeded in reducing canteen waste from 20 to just 2 bags a day. The school also collects batteries, electronics, and glasses for recycling.

This is a primary school, so if they can do all of this, older students certainly can!

These Lothrop School pupils are putting their used containers into recycling bins.

Keep up the good work

Once you have a recycling scheme up and running, you'll want to ensure it keeps going. What incentives can you use? At Mount Gambier High School, South Australia, students who help to recycle can get AUD$1 (66p) vouchers to use in the canteen, with "triple pay" if they help out after school. Students who have worked particularly hard for the recycling programme can even win a cinema pass.

Boys at Downton Value School in Los Angeles are collecting food for the compost bin after lunch. The school also grows vegetables in their garden and in a greenhouse.

"Most classrooms and office areas have a box for cardboard [recycling]. Twice a term (more often in the office areas) and at the end of the year, we empty the boxes into the big white SITA dumpster."

Timothy Z, Portside Christian School, South Australia

Being green - summing up

- Cut waste by reducing, reusing, and recycling.
- Focus on reducing use of paper and plastic products.
- Reuse paper for rough work or art projects.
- Take charge of recycling and encourage others.

Eco-friendly food

What fast and simple changes can you make so your food and drink are more eco-friendly, cheaper, and better for you? Firstly, assess yourself! Are you wasteful or waste-aware?

Check the **disposable** items below. How does your packed lunch fare?
- sandwich in a card or plastic box
- salad in a plastic box
- pre-packed pie
- crisps, bars, or cakes in plastic packaging
- pot of yoghurt
- carton or bottle of drink
- plastic cutlery
- plastic bags

If you have a high score of disposable items in your lunch, consider the ideas below. Or if you're having pasta or rice for supper, why not make a little extra to keep for lunch the next day?

1. Pick a carbohydrate (bread, pasta, couscous, rice).
2. Choose fresh vegetables in season or tinned vegetables.
3. Add protein (prepared meat, tinned fish, cheese, cooked pulses).
4. Pack or chop fruit into natural yoghurt (from a large carton).
5. Put your meal and yoghurt into food containers.
6. Pour juice or water into a drinks bottle (strong plastic or metal).

All the plastic food containers in this healthy packed lunch can be reused again and again.

Fresh fruit needs no preparation – just pop it in your lunch box.

Eco snacks

Of course, it can be hard to be organized enough to prepare food every day. An eco tuck shop can help. At Ithaca Creek State Primary School, Australia, the tuck shop staff prepare sandwiches and salads with fresh ingredients – some of the produce comes from the school garden. They minimize food waste by only making meals or sandwiches when they are ordered. Any leftover food goes in the **wormery** along with fruit and vegetable peelings. The liquid from the wormery fertilizes the garden, and the whole cycle begins again!

Processed organic foods

Ready-made **organic** meals and snacks are convenient, but are they better for the environment?
- Pros: the ingredients are products of **organic farming**, which does not use chemical **fertilizers** that can harm wildlife.
- Cons: processing food requires a large amount of energy. Once produced, processed foods are packaged, transported, and often chilled in a refrigerator – just like non-organic foods.

Think about your drink

There's nothing wrong with buying a drink every now and again when you're out and about. However, although some bottled drinks are healthy, many contain a large amount of sugar and additives, and they are not cheap. Also, packaging, transporting, and refrigerating the beverages come at a cost to the environment.

So, how can you cut down on costs and waste but stay hydrated and healthy? If you live in an economically developed country such as the United Kingdom, your home will have a fresh water supply – and it's probably cleaner and safer than bottled water. In some areas, the water is safe but does not taste good. You could talk to your family about buying a water filter to make tap water taste better.

Eco Impact

A US report in 2010 showed that:

- 50 per cent of bottled water is actually tap water in a plastic bottle.
- 75 per cent of the bottles are thrown away, not recycled.
- The plastic in some bottles leaches (leaks) a substance called phthalate into the water. Some studies have linked this chemical with hormonal problems in people.
- Bottled water goes through fewer safety tests than tap water.
- Bottled water costs 100 times as much as tap water! Bottled water typically costs just over $1 for 3.8 litres (nearly 7 pints) and much more when you buy smaller bottles. Water from the tap costs about 1c per 3.8 litres.

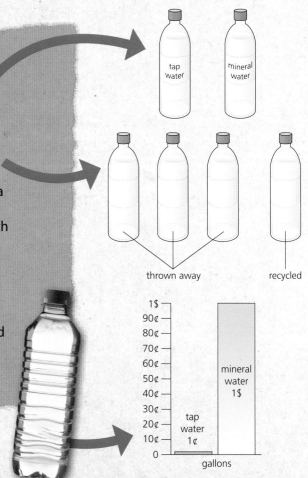

40

Be smart with smoothies

Do you like fruit smoothies or yoghurt drinks? You could save cash and packaging by filling up a drink bottle from a large bottle at home instead of buying small bottles. Even better, why not make your own smoothie with a blender? Fresh soft fruit in season is tasty or you can use tinned fruit. Bananas are great whizzed with natural yoghurt. It's easy and cheap to make your own smoothies.

Smoothie

You will need:

A few pieces of fruit, ideally two or three types, either fresh, tinned, or a mixture

About 250 ml (8.8 fl oz) of fruit juice, either fresh or from concentrate

A few ice cubes or some cold water

Method:

1. Wash and chop any fresh fruit into small pieces.

2. Put all the ingredients in a blender and whizz for about 30 seconds, until the mixture is smooth.

3. Add more juice or water if the smoothie is too thick.

4. If you have any left over, pour it into an ice lolly mould and freeze to make a healthy, eco-friendly summer treat.

Growing food

This is a cheap and easy way to grow food at school – even if there are no flower beds! Cylinder gardening uses containers that can be placed almost anywhere. You don't need any gardening experience and the preparation is simple. Why not give it a go?

Make a cylinder garden

You will need:

At least one 23-litre (5-gallon) bucket of the type used to transport food
 (you could ask a local café to supply clean buckets)
Potting soil
Vegetable seeds
Fertilizer

Method:

1. Work out where to place your cylinder garden. You can position it on top of soil or on a man-made surface, such as concrete. Try to find an area that will receive at least six to eight hours of sunlight and is close to a source of water.

2. Research vegetables that will grow during the season you're in. If you're gardening at school, look for varieties that you can harvest within a school term – 30 to 90 days. Search for compact varieties that can grow in a small space. The vegetables mentioned on page 47 are suitable for cylinder gardening, as are beans, carrots, parsley, peas, or tomatoes.

3. Cut off the bottom of the bucket and discard it. Then cut the rest of the bucket in half. You may need to ask an adult to help you. Now you have two cylinders. (NB If you are placing the bucket on concrete, it's better not to cut it but to ask an adult to drill drainage holes in the bottom.)

4. Put the cylinders in position.

5. Fill them with potting soil and mix in some fertilizer.

6. Plant your seeds, following the instructions on the packet for spacing, and water gently.

7. Monitor the seedlings as they grow, watering to keep moist and adding fertilizer regularly. **Thin out** the seedlings if they are squashed together.

Source: KidsGardening, www.kidsgardening.org

Food miles

Growing your own vegetables reduces **food miles**. The principle behind food miles is that the further away your food is produced, the worse for the environment. However, bear in mind that beans produced locally using oil-based fertilizers and ploughed by diesel tractors could be worse than beans grown by less energy-intensive methods abroad. Storing local food for a long time to be eaten out of season can also use up a lot of energy.

Being green - summing up
- Make eco-friendly packed meals and snacks.
- Stay hydrated by drinking tap water and home-made smoothies.
- Grow your own food in a cylinder garden.

Nature and biodiversity

Why would you bother encouraging nature and biodiversity at school? Well, you spend a lot of time at school so it's worth making your school grounds more attractive. Most students find nature and outdoor education programmes engaging and enjoyable. Also, a school nature project can be large enough to make a difference to local wildlife.

Small creatures such as bees, beetles, spiders, and snails form an essential part of the food chain. Solitary bees are essential for pollinating flowers; spiders eat insect pests; snails provide food for birds and other animals, such as hedgehogs. Looking after these small creatures is important, but few modern gardens have natural areas where they can shelter. So, how about making a bug hotel in the autumn to keep the insects and snails snug during winter?

Make a bug hotel

You will need:

1 square metre (10 square feet) of plastic mesh or chicken wire
Plastic-covered garden wire, twine, or garden string
Several dead plant stems or twigs
Pile of fallen autumn leaves
Flat piece of wood or plastic (big enough to cover the top end
  of the mesh when it has been made into a tube)
Two or three large rocks
A few tent pegs

Did you know?
- We need insects to produce honey, chocolate, coffee, and silk.
- Insects are a vital food source for birds and animals.
- 90 per cent of wild flowers could be threatened with extinction (being wiped out) if there were no insects to pollinate them.

Method:

1. Decide where to put your bug hotel. A quiet corner in the shade is best.

2. Curl the plastic mesh or chicken wire into a tube. Tie it in place using four twists of garden wire.

3. Poke some dead plant stems or twigs through the sides of the cylinder at the bottom. They should overlap to form a mesh, which will stop the leaves from falling out of the bottom if you move the bug hotel. They will also stop the leaves from touching the ground and becoming damp.

4. Now loosely fill the cylinder with dead leaves.

5. Use the piece of wood to make a lid. Place rocks on top to keep it secure.

6. If your bug hotel is in a windy position, you can pin the cylinder to the ground using tent pegs.

Source: Buglife, www.buglife.org.uk

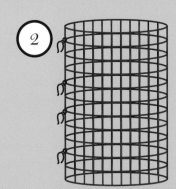

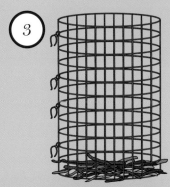

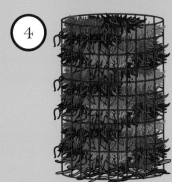

Make the most of your space

This raised bed is perfect for growing a variety of vegetables as well as wild flowers to attract wildlife. It's handy if you have a concrete patio or a small garden.

Build a no-dig raised garden bed

You will need:

Four planks of recycled wood to make a rectangle for the bed. Any length from 1 m (3 ft) upwards is fine. The depth should be at least 15 cm (6 in).
4 brackets, and galvanized screws to secure them
Several old cardboard boxes, more than enough to cover the base of the bed
Several old newspapers
A wheelbarrow or large tub for wetting the newspaper
Lucerne (alfalfa) hay
Manure
Straw
Some potting compost

Method:

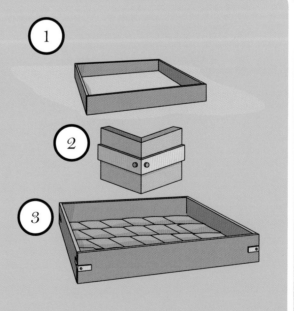

1. Decide where to place the bed — either on bare earth or grass. Lay out the planks of wood.

2. Place brackets over the corners where the planks meet and screw them in. You may need an adult to help.

3. Lay the cardboard on the base of the bed, making sure it overlaps.

4. Put the newspaper in a wheelbarrow or large plastic tub and pour some water over it.

5. Spread the wet newspaper over the cardboard, making sure the layers overlap by one-third of their size. Make sure the entire surface is covered to cut out the light. The cardboard and paper will rot down into the soil.

6. Add a layer of lucerne hay. This will feed the soil as it breaks down.

7. Add a thin layer of manure.

8. Lastly, add a layer of straw. This adds **nutrients** and acts as a mulch, keeping plants warm in winter and holding in moisture in summer.

9. Make small holes in the top layer of straw to make space for your plants. Add a handful of potting compost in each hole before putting in the plants.

Source: No Dig Vegetable Garden, www.no-dig-vegetablegarden.com

Easy-to-grow veggies

You can plant these vegetables directly in your raised bed:

- Lettuce: try "cut and come again" varieties. Once the lettuces are big, just cut off what you need and leave them to continue growing.
- Radishes: these don't need much care. You may need to thin them out if the seedlings sprout too close together.
- Spinach: the easiest to grow is spinach beet. You can pick off leaves, and the plant will keep growing.
- Chard: similar to spinach, and attractive with colourful red stems.
- Onions: it's simplest to plant onion sets, which are tiny onions.
- Potatoes: easy to grow but need plenty of water.

Bringing it together:
Kent Meridian High School

Kent Meridian High School in Kent, Washington, USA, is a Bronze level eco-school and part of the Cool School Challenge, an environmental programme.

For the Cool School Challenge, Environmental Science teacher Dianne Thompson and her pupils carried out an energy review. Pupil Asha Salim reports: "The students and Mrs Thompson's environmental science class go into the other classes and have a one-on-one discussion with the teachers about how much energy they're using and what they can do to reduce it." The pupils then offer tips to the teachers on how to cut down their energy use. In a few months' time, they go back and see how much energy those teachers have saved.

The students also tackle water waste. First they undertake a water assessment, going around the school looking for leaking taps. They produce a report for the caretaker and then the head. The last time they did this, they discovered six leaking taps that needed repairing.

This urban garden has been created by cleverly stacking wooden beds to make the best use of the available space and light.

Strawberries make a great addition to an edible garden.

Recycling is an essential element of the programme. Edros Palisoc describes recycling at Kent Meridian. "We recycle in the whole school … At lunch we have students who monitor the kids who have lunch to tell them which items are recyclable."

The school has a garden that attracts all kinds of wildlife, including songbirds, hummingbirds, and butterflies. There is a pond which contains fish. There is also an edible garden. As Deven Moss explains, "The edible garden is … being used for the cooking class. They can use the food there instead of having to find produce elsewhere to use." No **pesticides** are used to grow the crops.

This case study shows how many people in the school working together have succeeded in reducing energy use and water waste, increasing recycling, and encouraging wildlife. They are eco stars!

Being green - summing up

- Take part in school nature programmes.
- Make a bug hotel to attract insects.
- Build a raised bed to grow vegetables and wild flowers.
- Many schools around the world have gone green. Maybe your school can, too!

49

Quiz

Are you an eco star or an energy guzzler? Do this quiz to find out!
See page 55 for the results.

1. **When you're at home in the winter, do you . . .**
   a) crank up the heating so it's as hot as a sauna?
   b) keep the heating on all the time to keep the house warm?
   c) put the heating on for a few hours a day, and wear a cosy
      jumper or snuggle up with a warm blanket if you're cold?

2. **In your house, do you switch off lights and gadgets as soon as
   you've finished using them?**
   a) No, I leave them on in case someone else wants to use them.
   b) I turn off the lights but leave gadgets on standby so it's less
      effort to turn them on again later.
   c) Yes, I turn everything off – it's a waste of energy otherwise.

3. **Do you use the shower or bath?**
   a) There's nothing like a long, hot soak in a deep bath!
   b) I use the shower but I like a long, luxurious one.
   c) I have a quick, refreshing shower to save time and energy.

4. **How do you use water when you brush your teeth?**
   a) I run the tap while I'm brushing – it saves effort!
   b) I run the tap to wash my toothbrush and rinse my mouth.
   c) I fill a cup with water to rinse my mouth and the toothbrush.

5. **Are you an eco shopper?**
   a) Shopaholic more like! I have no willpower to resist the latest
      gadgets and accessories.
   b) I try to buy just the items I really need.
   c) I love rummaging in charity shops and rarely buy new goods.

6. How much do you recycle?

a) I don't bother. It's not going to change the world, is it?

b) I recycle paper, card, tins, and bottles.

c) Almost everything – I'm a total expert. I even know where to take old DVDs and batteries for recycling.

7. Do you have green fingers?

a) What, hang around in a muddy plot in the wind and rain? You've got to be joking.

b) I've tried growing some plants at home but they usually die.

c) Yes! I know how to look after plants and can raise easy-to-grow vegetables and herbs.

8. If you buy food or snacks when you're out, what do you do with the packaging?

a) I chuck it in the bin if there's one right there, otherwise on the ground.

b) I look for a bin or a recycling container.

c) I keep the packaging to wash and recycle once I get home.

9. How do you mostly travel around?

a) I like being driven around. I hate getting cold and wet when the weather's bad.

b) I sometimes get a lift in the car but I use the bus, walk, or cycle to some places.

c) I rarely go anywhere by car. I walk, cycle, or use public transport.

10. If you need to take a packed meal . . .

a) I buy everything pre-packaged to save time.

b) I make a sandwich or some pasta and take a carton of juice and a yoghurt or snack bar for convenience.

c) I make a sandwich or take some tasty cooked food from the fridge and some fresh fruit.

Glossary

biodiversity variety of plants and animals in a particular habitat or the world

climate change rising temperatures worldwide, caused by the increase of greenhouse gases in the atmosphere that trap the Sun's heat

compact fluorescent light bulb energy-saving light bulb. It is more efficient than an incandescent light bulb and lasts much longer.

conservation protecting wild habitats and their plants and animals

disposable made to be thrown away after being used once

draught proofing blocking up unwanted gaps that let in cold air, in order to save energy

energy-efficient using as little energy as possible for a task

fertilizer product added to soil or water to provide extra nutrients to help plants to grow

floodplain area of flat land alongside a river that regularly becomes flooded

flow meter bag bag with markings to measure the volume of water flowing in from a tap or shower

flow rate amount of liquid that flows in a given time, for example, 5 litres per minute

flow restrictor gadget designed to limit the amount of liquid that flows out of a tap or shower

food miles distance that foods travel from the point of origin to your table

fossil fuel energy source such as coal, gas, and oil, which was formed over millions of years from the remains of animals or plants

incandescent light bulb type of light bulb commonly used in homes. It is not energy efficient and is gradually being phased out.

kilowatt hour measurement of electricity use over an hour. A kilowatt hour is when you use 1,000 watts of energy in an hour, for example, using a 1,000-watt oven for one hour.

landfill area of land where large amounts of waste material are buried under the earth

lumens measurement of the amount of visible light a bulb gives out

mulch organic matter, such as leaves, straw, or bark chippings that is placed around the base of plants to improve the quality of the soil

nectar-rich rich in nectar, a sweet liquid produced by flowers and collected by bees for making honey

non-governmental organization non-profit organization that is not part of the government and works to help people

nutrient chemical that nourishes living things

organic produced without using man-made chemicals

organic farming method of farming that minimizes the use of harmful chemical fertilizers and pesticides. Organic farming is also known as all-natural farming.

pesticide chemical used to kill insects or other organisms that are harmful to crops

pollinate to put pollen into a plant so that it produces seeds

prevailing wind wind from the direction that is most common in a particular place or season

public liability insurance insurance to cover a group or event in case they have to pay out money to members of the public because of an injury or damage to their property

risk assessment careful examination of what could cause harm to people

sustainable way of doing something that does not use up too many natural resources or pollute the environment

thermal imaging measuring the surface temperature, for example of a house, so people can work out where heat is being lost

thin out remove weaker seedlings to allow space for the stronger ones to grow well

watt unit of power that measures the rate of using electricity

wind turbine huge fan that turns the moving energy of the wind into useful energy

wormery compost bin containing worms that are particularly effective at breaking down food waste, including cooked food

Find out more

Further reading

47 Things You Can Do for the Environment, Lexi Petronis, Karen Macklin, Jill Buck (Connections Book Publishing Ltd, 2012)

Generation Green: The Ultimate Teen Guide to Living an Eco-Friendly Life, Linda and Tosh Sivertsen (Simon Pulse, 2008)

Living Green: The Ultimate Teen Guide (It Happened to Me), Kathlyn Gay (Scarecrow Press, 2012)

The Eco-Student's Guide to Being Green at School, J. Angelique Johnson (Picture Window Books, 2010)

The Green Teen: The Eco-Friendly Teen's Guide to Saving the Planet, Jenn Savedge (New Society Publishers, 2009)

The Young Activist's Guide to Building a Green Movement and Changing the World, Sharon J. Smith (Ten Speed Press, 2011)

Websites

www.direct.gov.uk/en/environmentandgreenerliving/ greenercommunityandwork/dg_064439
Find out how to be greener in your community.

www.eco-schools.org
This is the website for the international Eco-Schools campaign.

www.keepbritaintidy.org/ecoschools
www.ecoschoolsscotland.org
www.eco-schoolswales.org
These are the Eco-Schools websites for England, Scotland, and Wales.

www.energysavingtrust.org.uk/In-your-home/Water
See the Energy Saving Trust's advice for saving water.

globalstewards.org
This website has a list of ways to reduce, reuse, and recycle.

www.keepbritaintidy.org
Details about the national campaign against litter.

www.wow.sa.gov.au
This Australian site focuses on school campaigns to cut waste.

DVDs

Food, Inc., director Robert Kenner (Dogwoof, 2010)

The Age of Stupid, director Franny Armstrong (Dogwoof, 2009)

The Truth about Climate Change, presenter David Attenborough
   (Eureka Entertainment, 2008)

More topics to research

Once you've read this book, you might like to research Eco-Schools in
your area – perhaps you could link up with them and share ideas? It
could be exciting to make contact with a school in another country,
too. You may also want to find out what your local council is doing
to protect the environment. Perhaps your eco group could come up
with suggestions for how to promote eco policies to young people?

Answers to panel question (page 28):
You would need to buy about 21 bulbs that last 850 hours to get 18,000 hours
of service (21 x 850 = 17,850 hours). Those 21 bulbs will cost you £75.60. So the
£40 bulb is a better buy.

Answers to quiz (pages 50–51):
Mostly As:
Sounds like you're an energy guzzler but at least you're aware of it. Pick just
a couple of ideas from this book and start being a little more eco-friendly.

Mostly Bs:
You're clearly making an effort. Look for a few ideas in this book to do more.

Mostly Cs:
You're an eco star! Keep up the good work and spread the message to others.

Index